CASE STUDIES

Picking
A Winner

Taking Part in Regional and National Book Awards

Yorkshire & Humberside SLA Branch

Edited by
Sally Dring and Geoff Dubber

School Library Association

Acknowledgements

The SLA's Publications Team of Geoff Dubber, Richard Leveridge and Jane Cooper would like to thank all the contributors from the SLA's Yorkshire & Humberside branch and other colleagues in public library services in the area, especially our own Board member and stalwart member of the Publications Group, Sally Dring, who gathered these case studies from her colleagues and undertook the initial administration work and text edit and wrote the introduction.

Published by

School Library Association
1 Pine Court, Kembrey Park
Swindon SN2 8AD

Tel: 01793 530166 Fax: 01793 481182
E-mail: info@sla.org.uk
Web: www.sla.org.uk

Registered Charity Nos: 313660 and SC039453

ISBN: 978-1-903446-83-6

Printed by Holywell Press, Oxford

Contents

Contents

Please note:

The internet addresses (URLs) given in this book were correct at the
time of going to press. However, due to the dynamic nature of the
internet, web addresses and content may have changed or ceased to
exist since publication. While we regret any inconvenience this may
cause readers, no responsibility for any such changes can be accepted
by the authors, editors or publisher.

Introduction

Showcasing Book Awards for School Libraries

Sally Dring

Learning Resources Manager and Literacy & Numeracy Coordinator at Ripon School, Chair of the SLA Yorks & Humberside branch and SLA Board member 2009–2012 and 2013 to date

At a recent training day organised by the Yorkshire and Humberside branch of the School Library Association, the afternoon session consisted of regional members sharing examples of good practice. It was obvious that school librarians in the region were forging ahead with finding creative ways to promote reading for pleasure and to include all areas of their communities.

In this publication we showcase several different case studies:

- Lyn Hopson and Lesley Hurworth describe the growth of the Doncaster Book Award from the seed of an idea to a huge award scheme involving public libraries, primary and secondary schools and other community organisations, now in its tenth year.

- At Brayton High School, Jean Corson has used the CILIP Carnegie Shadowing Scheme to create a close link with the local public library customer services centre and another high school.

- In Sheffield, Paul Register spotted a gap in the market and filled it neatly by creating the Stan Lee Excelsior Award for graphic and manga novels.

- Alison Roberts outlines Calderdale Children's Book of the Year Awards – an excellent collaboration between Discover, the Children's and Education Service in Libraries, Museums and Arts and local primary and secondary schools.

- Rossett School in Harrogate takes part in book testing for the Red House Children's Book Award (RHCBA) and Jo Huet, their Librarian, explains how this benefits the students.

- The Leeds Book Awards, run by Leeds public library service and the Schools Library Service have been running for seven years and Pauline Thresh outlines how they were created to give Children and Young People a greater voice in voting for their favourite books.

- In Doncaster Lynne Coppendale, Librarian at Danum Academy, describes how she uses the Greenaway Shadowing scheme both in school and as a transition activity with local primaries.

- The James Reckitt Hull Children's Book Award is named after a business pioneer and philanthropist whose bequest funds the award scheme, as Christine Hill explains.

- and Monica O'Neill from Ossett Academy and her colleague Lesley Marshall from Wakefield Schools Library Service outline their useful collaboration for the Wakefield Riveting Reads Book Awards.

We hope this publication will give you the inspiration to see what schemes are available in your own area and, if there aren't any, maybe you could consider setting up your own. These case studies only serve to confirm what we already know – many of you out there are doing wonderful things, and going to extraordinary lengths, to nurture that love of reading in your students.

Case Study 1

Doncaster Book Award: Growing and Thriving

Lyn Hopson and Lesley Hurworth

Doncaster Book Awards Ltd

Doncaster Book Award (DBA) is just ending its tenth year and is going from strength to strength.

It first began in 2004, with a small group of Doncaster school librarians who had been working together very successfully for a few years on projects such as the Carnegie Award shadowing scheme. We and our students enjoyed this immensely, but increasingly we found students were unhappy with the judges' choice of winner, and would express their dissatisfaction loudly!

We began to consider trying to set up our own book award scheme that would put them in the driving seat, and, after taking advice from other local book award organisers, decided to have a go. In the first year 15 secondary schools agreed to take part. It was great fun, and the students were extremely enthusiastic. Our success encouraged others to get on board, and numbers have grown every year, so that now over 70 local schools participate.

Aims of the Award

The DBA's main aims, as listed here, were agreed early on, and have remained constant throughout. They are:

- To promote reading for pleasure and extend reading choices
- To create an award that was local and put the young people of Doncaster in control
- To raise the profile of literacy and libraries in Doncaster
- To promote positive social interaction and debate and create a sense of community.

Award Timetable

We also had to agree a time-frame, and decided to run our award from October – March, thus avoiding a clash with Carnegie/Greenaway and SATS. We wanted the books, from the long-list stage and throughout, to be the children's choices. So, working with our local public library service, we obtained their borrowing statistics to establish the most popular titles published the previous year up to the end of June. We took into consideration things like length of time since publication to ensure a level playing field, and came up with our first long list of 25 books. We have since learnt that 25 books is too many, so reduced it to 20. Also, last year and for this forthcoming year, due to funding and staffing cuts in the public libraries, our statistics have been obtained from our local Waterstones, but the process itself remains essentially the same. Also last year, for the first time we have introduced separate primary and secondary lists, and a classics list, an attempt to revitalise the scheme that has proved immensely popular. All three lists can be read and voted for by all age groups, or schools/individuals can choose to focus on just one of the lists.

Following our launch, the children read and review the books, posting their reviews and comments on our interactive website, www.doncasterbookaward.net. They vote in early January for the shortlist, then in mid-March for the overall winners. The website itself was designed jointly by a group of young people from various participating schools, and we also ran inter-school competitions to design our logo and strapline, so it really is our young people's award in every sense. The timetable acts as a framework; we hold a launch event every October and a grand Finale in March, and in between run a variety of events and activities, all publicised via the website and free to attend. These include author events, drama and creative writing workshops, poetry slams, illustration workshops, 'Murder in the Library', visits to Seven Stories, and last year two days of 'Alice in Wonderland' themed 'Play in a Day' events led by a local theatre company and held in a local museum, Cusworth Hall. Schools can choose how much involvement they want to have, from simply having the books in their libraries and classrooms, to participating in all of our events and activities. Even children whose schools are not involved can still post reviews and comments, vote via Waterstones and, since their parents can contact us directly through the website, join in with events and activities happening in the holidays or at weekends. We are a completely inclusive award!

Funding

Once we had settled on our aims and planned our framework, the next key priority was to obtain funding. As well as agreeing to share resources between schools, we first approached our local education authority, and were initially awarded funds from their borough-wide 'Gifted and Talented' funding stream. We then invited senior LEA staff and various local dignitaries, including the Mayor, to our first Finale. Impressed by the evident enthusiasm and excitement we had generated around books and reading, the Mayor offered us more funding if we invited primaries to participate the next year. We duly did so, and got the money, another £1,000. The LEA also agreed at this stage to provide sufficient funding for the next few years. Their English consultants, both primary and secondary were really impressed with the scheme, and even funded and worked with us to produce a booklet about the DBA that was sent to other authorities as an example of good practice.

Keeping the Momentum Going

However, around three years ago, with cuts in public funding beginning to bite, we recognised there was a real need to look for other funding sources if the DBA was to continue. This was a good move, as Doncaster's LEA has now shrunk massively, and the consultants' roles have disappeared entirely. Central funding streams, like the Literacy Strategy, Aim Higher and Gifted and Talented were also, we knew, going to disappear. Fortuitously, at around this time Lesley and I were invited to attend an event for local organisations in North Doncaster, run by a Development Trust and focused on third sector, i.e. charitable and voluntary groups. This truly was a 'Eureka' moment as it opened our eyes to a whole new funding arena. However, it also highlighted the fact that our current organisational structure would not allow us access to any of these 'pots' and that we needed to address the situation urgently.

It was time to do some research. We looked on-line at the various options, and then Lesley and I made an appointment with Doncaster CVS, an umbrella organisation offering support to third sector groups. These exist in most areas. They gave us lots of advice, including a free session with a solicitor, and we found that if we wanted to become a Social Enterprise Company, we could actually bid for funding to cover the legal incorporation process. We did so and were successful. As a committee, we had decided to adopt the model of a not-for-profit Social Enterprise Company Limited by Guarantee and, in October 2010, Doncaster Book Awards Ltd was born. Rather than a group of like-minded people working together, things are now much more formally structured. Each of us has a legal contract detailing our duties and responsibilities, and we also have to file accounts and Annual Reports at Companies House. However the benefits have been huge. The CVS provided training and advice and also links to fund-holders we could now approach, such as the Lottery, the Coalfields Regeneration Trust and the Arts Council. We attended presentations and surgeries run by funders and began to apply, and last year succeeded in obtaining around £20,000!

This amount of funding allowed us to run bigger and better events. It has also meant that some publishers/authors began to approach us if they were intending to come to the area, knowing that we had the capacity to arrange large events. Waterstones too have asked us to get involved in events they wanted to run, such as a poetry event in-store, and a joint visit from author Tom Palmer and Labour Leader Ed Milliband. Two years ago we ran an event at Doncaster Racecourse with Charlie Higson speaking to 450 students and with BBC television and radio in attendance. Our Finale that year was even more spectacular. We went for an 'Olympics' theme and 500 young people came to the Keepmoat athletics stadium to take part in book-themed races, break the World Reading Relay Record (for two weeks at least!) and listen to authors Tanya Landman, Phillip Ardagh and Gareth Jones speak about their work. The authors loved the excitement on the day and praised our innovative approach on their websites. Phillip Ardagh actually came back again last year to speak at our launch event in the Doncaster Civic Theatre, much to the delight of the audience, who loved his zany humour. The Lottery, who funded the Keepmoat event, were delighted by the scale of the project and made a film of the Finale event for their website! (It can be viewed from our DBA 'Events' page.) In June 2013, for our Finale, we held a massive 'Mad Hatters Tea Party' event in the grounds of Cusworth Hall. Around 350 students attended and took part in a series of workshops, watched a drama performance, met winning secondary author Cathy Cassidy and viewed two 'Oscars style' acceptance videos from our other winners, Liz Pichon and John Boyne. We even had a competition for each school to design a teapot and the fabulous entries can be viewed on the website. It was a magical day.

However, we cannot afford to rest on our laurels and the efforts to obtain funding are constant and on-going. As a committee, we meet in our own time and, although our events often take place during school time, this is not always the case. We do sometimes work at weekends and in the holidays, all on a completely voluntary and unpaid basis. We also mainly work on the organisational and administrative tasks relating to the DBA in our own time. We feel that all of this is very worthwhile and are extremely proud of the project. As secondary librarians, the Doncaster Book Award allows our students to participate in fantastic events and to meet authors that our individual school budgets simply would not cover. In addition, through the DBA, our students get the chance to meet and work with students from other schools and to build understanding and friendships around a shared love of books. As a transition project too it is fantastic, providing lots of opportunities for secondary schools to work with their local primaries in a positive and fun way. It has been a fantastic way to promote reading for pleasure throughout our whole community.

Should anyone reading this case study have any questions about the DBA, Lesley and I are both very happy to provide further information on request, and our details can be obtained from the website. We hope to be around for some time to come and that the Doncaster Book Award will continue to grow and thrive. Watch this space!

To find out more about the Doncaster Book Award, visit the official website: www.doncasterbookaward.net

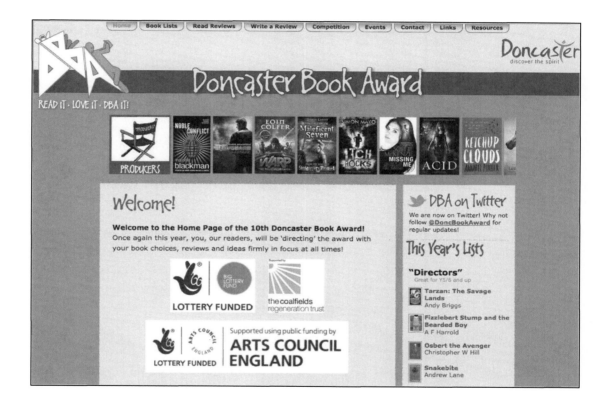

Case Study 2

Shadowing the CILIP Carnegie Award at Brayton High School

Jean Corson

LRC Manager at Brayton High School, Selby, North Yorkshire

Shadowing the CILIP Carnegie Award is a wonderful way to introduce new book themes and genres to pupils and there are hundreds of schools and reading groups, worldwide, who join the shadowing process every year. At Brayton High School, here in Selby, we work closely with our near neighbours, Lesley Cobb, LRC Manager at Selby High School, and Voirrey Whittaker who represents Selby Library and Customer Services Centre. This collaboration works well and all concerned use this approach to enhance the experiences that we provide for the young people of the town.

Working with two external organisations adds an extra dimension to the shadowing experience but does bring some extra work in organisation. It is important to liaise with each other and agree suitable dates for our meetings and, as this involves taking the pupils out of lessons, we need to have the permission of our respective head teachers. Luckily, both are very supportive and are aware of the high value that shadowing this award can have in awakening the high order, critical thinking skills which are vitally important to our pupils.

'Absolutely Jean. It's an excellent activity. Please proceed.'

This was the response of Mike Roper, Headteacher at Brayton High School, when asked for permission to begin the shadowing process in 2013.

Getting Going

Permission received, we now begin to choose the pupils who would benefit from becoming involved. At Brayton we choose the shadowers from Year 9 (aged 14) and avoid pupils from Years 10 and 11, who are preparing for their GCSEs.

We are also aware that as some of the books can have grown up themes and language, this might not be a suitable activity for the younger pupils! We like to work with up to 12 pupils from each school and invite an English teacher to become involved, although it has been known for us to use an ICT teacher in support.

The next few weeks are rather quiet and we use this time to enthuse the young people and make sure that they are up for the challenge. However, if your name is Mrs Cobb, LRC Manager at Selby High, you also use this time to study the longlist and try to forecast what books will make the shortlist and get reading!

A typical meeting schedule would look like this:

1. 12th March – Launch at Selby Library and Customer Services Centre

2. 29th April – Meeting at Brayton High School

3. 24th May – Meeting at Selby High School

4. 19th June – Winner announced at Selby Library and Customer Services Centre

As our shadowing experience involves taking the pupils off site, it is at this point that the dreaded risk assessment should be tackled, and the assistance and patience of our Education Visits Co-ordinator is much appreciated. The LEA has strict policies to follow when young people are taken off site, part of which is obtaining written parental consent as well as an up to date medical form in case of emergencies.

Having received permission, chosen the shadowers, agreed a meeting schedule and completed the risk assessment, we need to arrange to buy the books. We use the award's official supplier who can guarantee to dispatch our order for delivery on the day that the shortlist is announced. We buy three sets of the shortlist which can cost around £180 and we consider ourselves lucky if we have any of the shortlisted books sitting on the shelves.

Finally, it is here. We have the confirmed shortlist and three copies of every shortlisted book! This is a very exciting moment which is shared with like-minded friends in the English Department. We get together in the LRC office to open the box and spend 15 minutes reading blurbs, oohing, aahing, groaning, touching the shiny new covers and smelling the newness of these lovely books. Very soon, however, this frivolity is banished and final preparations are made for our visit to Selby public library.

Preparation consists of cataloguing and protecting the stock for lending as well as printing the first few lines of each book onto plain A4 paper, giving no clues about the books whatsoever (all will soon become clear). Contact is made with the public library to book three internet linked computers, so that we can show the pupils the shadowing site and how to write their reviews.

The shadowing site is very easy to use. Lesley and I each have a user name and password, so that we can maintain our own sites, checking reviews and customising specific aspects of it. Take a look at www.ckg.org.uk for more information, including reviews from the previous year.

Visit 1:
Selby Library and Customer Services Centre

This visit takes place as soon as possible after the shortlist has been announced and for us, it is about a 20 minute walk through Selby town centre. As soon as we get there, we introduce ourselves and encourage the young people to do the same. Library staff are always helpful and keen to show the shadowers around the library, providing them with information about joining the library and how it can help with their studies and recreation. Copies of the shortlisted titles are bought as part of the North Yorkshire County Council (NYCC) stock specification, so even if they are not in stock at Selby library, they will be available from the NYCC libraries stock holdings.

We then find a quiet corner and read the prepared first lines of each novel, gauging the likes and dislikes of the group. Next, we introduce the books, read the blurbs and examine the front covers. Have opinions changed? Which books do we expect to enjoy reading and which books will become a chore?

It is important at this stage, to make the group aware of the Award Criteria, which are available on the shadowing website and are followed by the 'real' judges. These include areas such as plot construction, believable, well-rounded characters and the effectiveness of the narrative used throughout the story. After about 45 minutes we set off back to our respective schools with our first book to read.

> 'We are really keen to work alongside the high schools on this scheme. We have a lot of contact with children of primary school age but they tend to drift away at secondary level. This is a fantastic way to make contact with them again and a great reader development opportunity.'
> —Voirrey Whitaker, Senior Development Officer,
> North Yorkshire County Libraries

Visit 2:
Brayton High School

With the shadowing group out of their regular lesson, we await the arrival of the Selby High shadowers in the LRC. In preparation, the front cover of each book has been photocopied, a portable display board is ready, with a roll of double sided sticky tape available, but before we begin the debate, we share some refreshments with our visitors who have had a 15 minute walk. By now, we can see that some of the students are forming friendships and getting to know each other so we allow time for a short chat about things before we officially welcome the visitors who hopefully, include a representative from the public library.

This is a teacher-led, general debate focusing on our very early opinions, as it is unlikely that any of us will have read all of the books. The session leader will choose a front cover and start with the obvious 'who has read this one?' and, after encouraging the group to share opinions, we will decide (a bit like 'Play Your Cards Right') whether it should be placed top middle or bottom of the display board. This process is followed for every book and we end up with a visual chart, the results of which can be transferred to our shadowing sites and shown as a reading barometer. We also produce a reading barometer for a display in the LRC which tracks our progress and keeps the debate alive, especially when we have a controversial but majority decided outcome!

An example of how the Reading Barometer would look on the wall of the LRC showing our current favourite at the top with the least liked at the bottom. It is also nice to have a photo of the current Brayton High/Selby High shadowing group.

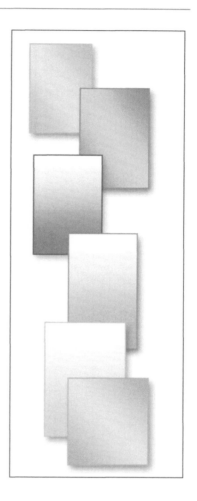

Visit 3:
Selby High School

In preparation for this meeting of the shadowing group, Lesley and I get together to write a quiz based on the shortlisted books which we have read. By this time, we are well into the shadowing period and, after some short telephone discussions, we are in a good position to do this as, between us, we can have all titles covered. On our arrival at Selby High, we again have some refreshment after our walk and then make up the teams. We make sure that each team has members from both schools and we also throw our supporting teachers into this mix by insisting that they make up team numbers and pit their wits against the pupils, leaving Lesley and I to be quiz masters extraordinaire!

> *'I love Carnegie. Jean and I have become good friends over the years that we have been taking part. It's not just for the kids; we also get a lot out of it.'*
> —Lesley Cobb, Learning Resource Centre Manager, Selby High School.

Although this is a fun activity with prizes, it also encourages the shadowers to continue with their reading and explore the genres and titles which they have chosen to avoid until now. It also exposes those who may not have spent as much time reading as they could have done and are falling a bit behind the others.

Visit 4:
The Awards Ceremony at Selby Library and Customer Services Centre

We like to organise our Brayton High/Selby High Awards Ceremony to coincide with the 'real' ceremony as it is happening in London, but this is likely to have an impact on our respective school timetables. However, as this is the only meeting which is non-negotiable, it is relatively easy to prise the shadowers away from their lessons with promises to class teachers that, as always, work missed will be caught up in the young person's own time.

Hopefully, by now, we will have read all of the shortlisted books which will allow us to make a reasonable judgement when casting our vote to decide our group winner and, for this process, we refer back to the criteria being used by the 'real' judges as they choose the winner.

To cast our vote, we use a prepared voting slip which prompts us to think about different aspects of the books and we continue to think about the criteria being used by the 'real 'judges. Favourite character; plot; setting; twist. Our votes are whisked away by a member of the public library team, who quickly collates the information and arrives back to share the outcome with us in the minutes before the official winner is revealed.

Carnegie Medal Voting Sheet

My favourite character is from _____

My favourite setting is from _____

My favourite plot is from _____

My favourite ending is from _____

My overall winner is from _____

By now, we are all keen to know which author has won the Carnegie Medal. Surely those 'real' judges, having read the exact same novels as us, will have reached the same, conclusion as us?

....and the winner of the Carnegie Medal is.............!

'What?' I hear with total indignation and disbelief! 'That can't be right. That book was rubbish.'

'Well actually, I liked it' comes the reply and the debate begins all over again.

Conclusion

To evaluate this experience, we need to think about cost and who has benefited. The total financial cost for this model is no more than £180, which will pay for enough copies of the shortlist, some prizes, photocopying, as well as refreshments. It would be nice to roll the experience out to more pupils but this would significantly raise costs.

At school, we can see an increased desire to read for pleasure, as the pupils are encouraged to explore new genres from authors who have produced good quality novels. The opportunity to practice their debating skills with a different audience is provided and the interaction with Selby High and the public library is a useful tool to provide evidence of working within the community.

The public library is able to promote services to the teenagers, encouraging them to join or re-join the library. Links with local high schools are reinforced and wider opportunities such as becoming young volunteers to help with the Summer Reading Challenge are promoted.

All in all it is easy to see that each organisation involved benefits greatly from the shared experience of shadowing the CILIP Carnegie Award.

Case Study 3

The Stan Lee Excelsior Award – A Case Study

Paul Register

Librarian, Ecclesfield School, Sheffield

What is the Stan Lee Excelsior Award?

Put simply, the Stan Lee Excelsior Award is the only nationwide book award for graphic novels and manga where 11–16 year olds decide the winner. The shortlist contains eight graphic novels that are chosen by me, Paul Register (award founder and organiser), with the help of the staff at Sheffield Space Centre (http://www.space-centre.co.uk/store/), the city's premier comic book store. The primary goal of this scheme is to encourage reading amongst teenagers. If it doesn't do that then it is failing. However, its secondary target is to raise the profile of graphic novels and manga amongst the librarians and teachers of the UK's schools. There are some amazing books out there that kids would love reading and deserve a spotlight throwing on them. Student readers rate and review each of the books on the shortlist, according to a variety of factors. But I'll go into that in greater detail later.

Genesis of the Award

In 2010, the organisers of the Sheffield Children's Book Awards (SCBA) decided, due to requests from school librarians, to have a special new category in their awards… for graphic novels and manga. The SCBA has been running since 1988 and for most of that time they've employed the format of Picture Books, Shorter Novels and Longer Novels. As they felt they didn't have the knowledge of graphics and manga to run a successful book shadowing scheme amongst the secondary schools – and they knew I had an interest and some knowledge in this field – they asked me to get involved. For me, it was something very different and exciting and a total labour of love. I put hours of my own time into it and thoroughly enjoyed doing so.

The big issues that needed addressing first were:

- Putting together a shortlist of titles
- Giving the award a cool and attractive name that would make kids say 'Wow! That sounds awesome!'

I've always been a believer in chance-taking – if you don't buy a raffle ticket, you don't win the prize. So when it came to naming this award I went right to the top and e-mailed Stan Lee himself – or his PA, at any rate.

Stan Lee's Involvement

For those of you who don't know who Stan Lee is, he is an absolute worldwide legend and a pop-culture icon. He is to superhero comics what Tolkien is to fantasy, what Bram Stoker is to horror and what Isaac Asimov is to science fiction. He really is that big a deal!

Stan Lee is considered by many to be the 'Godfather of Modern Comics'. His name is legendary within the comics and film industries - and beyond. His career in comic books spans more than 70 years, but has always been defined by Stan's dedication to the written word and commitment to excellence in the literary arts. In the 1960s, Stan was the writer who co-created *Spider-Man, Doctor Strange* (with Steve Ditko), *The X-Men, The Fantastic Four, Iron Man, The Hulk, Thor* (with Jack

Kirby), *Daredevil* (with Bill Everett) and many, many more iconic characters. His passion for teaching and sharing his craft is legendary and has spawned hundreds, if not thousands, of gifted writers and artists who have touched the lives of millions throughout the world. He is largely responsible for evolving Marvel Comics from a relatively small US publisher into the huge multinational corporation it is today. This is why Disney paid $4.24 billion for the company in 2009.

To my huge surprise, his PA actually replied and said that 'Stan the Man' (to use his colloquial nickname) would be delighted to have this award named after him! Obviously this was a massive coup! I was thrilled and so were the SCBA organisers. I'd managed to get the biggest name in comics to endorse and validate our new venture.

Independence and Evolution

Now is the time to skip ahead a few months. A shortlist of six titles was chosen by me and the SCBA's chief organiser, Jennie Wilson. That got whittled down to five due to one of the titles going out of print. The books were ordered and distributed to the schools where loads of students read them and voted for their favourite. At the awards ceremony at Sheffield City Hall, the manga title *Vampire Knight* was announced as the category winner, clearly a popular choice if the loud cheers were anything to go by. After the ceremony, I had many librarians and young people tell me how much they had enjoyed doing the reading (or 'shadowing', if you prefer) of this new 'Stan Lee Award'. I was absolutely delighted with such positive feedback and had already started planning in my head how to improve the system and the format for the following year.

After the SCBA dust had settled, I contacted the organisers and said 'Many thanks for allowing me to be involved in this project. I can't wait to do it again next year. I think, with some extra planning and a better shortlist, we can really make a big success of it!' However, they didn't see this new category for graphic novels and manga as anything other than a one-off. A 'guest' category, if you will.

Now, I fully appreciate that this is THEIR award and they've been doing things their way very successfully for years and years – I was just 'hired help'. I didn't take their decision personally and didn't hold any grudges... but I did disagree. I could sense that there was a need for something like this amongst the teenagers of Sheffield's schools. There was a hunger for it. Students who had previously felt that comics-reading wasn't 'proper reading' suddenly found their choices validated. Those that read comics (and generally preferred them over prose fiction) no longer felt quite so alone or embarrassed. There were kids at other schools reading the same stuff they were. There were even adults reading the same stuff they were! Their geeky hobby was being held up alongside the novels that their English teachers were championing – and they were holding their own. To scrap the award now and consign it to history seemed like a real opportunity wasted. It also seemed like a real shame to get Stan Lee's permission to use his name for a project that would only last for one year.

So I decided to see if I could do this alone. I went to see my Headteacher and I explained the project to him and how much funding I would need to run it across the secondary schools of Sheffield. He agreed that it was just the sort of project that we should be undertaking as part of our school's wider community commitments and gave me a sizeable budget to work with. I was able to buy a complete set of the shortlisted books for twelve of Sheffield's secondary schools. Further good news was to follow when the local Schools Library Service offered to match my funding – so those schools actually got two copies of each book.

Analysing the work that I myself and the SCBA organisers had done on this award in the past spotlighted **five key changes** I believed needed to be made right from the beginning:

1. Making it clear that this was going to be an **annual event**, not a one-off. I believed librarians would be more likely to commit to something like this if they could see it as something that had the potential to grow and evolve every year and not just fade away like so many initiatives do in schools.

2. Getting the students to **rate** each book straight after they've read it (giving marks out of 5 for *Story*, *Artwork*, *Characters* and *Dialogue*) instead of just voting for their favourite, with the option for a review too. This would keep the process simple for students whilst negating any inherent or subconscious favouritism they may feel towards books featuring better known characters. I also felt that rating instead of voting elicits a very instant and honest response from the reader and allows them to judge each book on its merits and in isolation.

3. Changing the name to the **Stan Lee Excelsior Award**. For those who don't know, Stan Lee's catchphrase is 'Excelsior!', a catchphrase he used (amongst others) in hundreds of Marvel comics across the sixties and seventies, usually in the narrative boxes at the end of stories and frequently in the letters pages. It is Latin for 'Ever Upward' and if that's a motto that's good enough for Stan then it's good enough for my award too.

4. Increasing the number of books on the shortlist from **six to eight** and raising the budget ceiling from **£50 to £75**. This has worked very well. It's a good amount to work with for librarians. £75 is perfectly affordable for most librarians and eight books allows a broad range of material to be chosen.

5.   Organising a big **awards ceremony** at the school. Awards ceremonies are fun and exciting. Students like them and they are relatively straightforward trips for school staff to organise. I wanted something to try and create a bridge between readers and creators. I wanted to show that no matter how fantastic a writer or artist might be, they were still human beings and were always happy to meet fans of their work.

As word of this exciting new award for graphic novels and manga spread across the internet and the school librarian community, other schools from outside Sheffield contacted me and asked if they could take part, including Carol Webb who had just been selected as the new SLA School Librarian of the Year. I explained to them that I unfortunately didn't have the funding to cover any schools from outside the city - and they were absolutely fine with that. They purchased their own books and took part in the Reading & Rating process in exactly the same way as all the Sheffield schools. In the end, I had 17 schools from across the UK involved!

The Shortlist and Reading & Rating Period

It's important to stress that I don't ever present the Excelsior Award as being something that makes grand claims about being able to pick the greatest graphic novel published in any given year. As far as I am concerned, it is as much a **reading scheme** as it is a book award. I don't know if the shortlists of other national book awards are deliberately designed to reflect a range of genres and writing styles but mine certainly is. The shortlisted books are chosen for their quality, their popularity and their variety of genre and artistic styles. The list must appeal to **all** types of students, across gender, race, reading ability and social class. There must be something for everybody on there.

The other main criteria for their inclusion on the shortlist is that the titles should be suitable for 11–16 year olds and must have been published in the previous calendar year. The shortlist is always announced in mid-December which makes it much simpler to compile a longlist from January to December. At the end of every month I look at all the new graphic novels that have come out that month, mainly using Amazon's website. If anything catches my eye (or if I had some prior knowledge of it) I add it to the longlist. The last three year's shortlists can all be found on the website.

The **Reading & Rating** period takes place over approximately a ten week period. This is the most active part of the whole process for students. They read one of the books on the shortlist and then fill in a Rating Form straight after. As I mentioned before, they give it marks out of five for *Story*, *Artwork*, *Characters* and *Dialogue* –

they do NOT vote for their favourite. The focus is very much on keeping it fun and simple with the actual reading at the top of the agenda. When the deadline day approaches, the participating schools simply post all their completed Rating Forms to me and I begin the long, slow process of compiling and analysing all the data and finding out the top three books.

There are also two other awards:

- The **True Believers Award** – for the school that returns the most Rating Forms.

- The **JABBICA** – which stands for *'Judge A Book By Its Cover Award'*. This is obviously for the book that is judged to have the most artistically impressive cover and is voted for only by the librarians and teachers. It is a simple way of helping them to feel involved in the process.

Other aspects and other new sub-awards may well appear in the future as the Excelsior Award evolves. Stagnation is not on the agenda!

The Ceremony

Part of the annual process is the organisation of the awards ceremony. Book awards always need a proper ceremony and I like to put on a good show for the kids and librarians that attend. This takes place at my school in Sheffield as we have a fantastic main hall with excellent facilities and the school isn't far from the M1. However, I am not going to go into too much detail about all that in this case study. As far as I have always been concerned, the ceremony is just 'the icing on the cake'. It should never detract from the reading or from the shortlist. I know that if I start planning any new shortlist with the awards ceremony in mind, I am losing my primary focus and I run the risk of producing a shortlist that is not chosen for the range and quality of reading it will engender in our students. The shortlist is the brain and spinal column of the whole project. If you wish to see how the awards ceremony works in more detail I would heartily recommend watching the videos (and seeing the galleries) on my website. These can be seen at http://www.excelsioraward.co.uk/ceremony.html. We have had some incredible special guests at the ceremony though. Comics people are extremely supportive and make little to no charge for their attendance. Over the last two years, I have had the likes of **Kev. F. Sutherland, Andy Diggle, Bryan Talbot, Ben Haggarty** and **Ian Churchill** (if you don't know who these guys are, you should Google them!) attend and even the Chairman of the Stan Lee Foundation – **Ted Adams III** – flew in from Washington for our first event! I also arrange for other stalls to be there (including a book stall provided by the Sheffield Space Centre, artwork stall and even a cupcake stall) and we have a big quiz and a raffle with some excellent prizes provided by a variety of different publishers, writers and artists. I try to create a sort of mini comic convention atmosphere and I think it's fair to say that the kids have an absolutely great time.

The Future

As I write this, the Stan Lee Excelsior Award has grown from a starting point of **17 schools** in 2011 to **77 schools** the following year. In 2013, **129 schools** signed up to participate in the award. We had our first schools from Wales and the Republic of Ireland take part and, truth be told, I would love to just see it grow and grow every year. I try to make it as simple and as fun and interesting for all involved – readers and organisers – as I possibly can. The website has made a big difference and the hosting of this comes out of my own pocket every month. I think of it as 'an investment in my career'. It's opened up many doors for me personally and professionally. I've given several talks about the Award to fellow librarians and to students at other schools. My Headteacher and my school are very supportive. And I've met some of my comics heroes, including (but certainly not limited to) Stan Lee himself! The man is 90 now and he still has amazing energy levels! He's totally inspirational.

I hope this case study has been an interesting read for you and given you an insight into what goes on behind the scenes of one guy running his own nationwide book award. If you have never taken part I hope it makes you want to participate next year. At the very least I hope it makes you want to pick up a graphic novel and have a look at it with fresh eyes and a new enthusiasm. Thank you for reading.

Case Study 4

Calderdale Children's Book of the Year Awards

Alison Roberts

Co-ordinator, Schools' Library and Resource Service, Discover, Calderdale Libraries

The annual Calderdale Children's Book of the Year Awards (CCBY) is held in Calderdale Central Library, Halifax, and has been running in its present format for about ten years. The award is the brainchild of Discover, the Children's and Education Service in Libraries, Museums and Arts. There are two parallel events, one for upper primary and one for younger secondary pupils. For the purposes of this article I will focus on the secondary event and the involvement of the high school librarians.

The event started off with 10 schools each sending 10 children and 2 staff to the Literary Lunch but growing popularity has led to us accommodating 12 and now 14 schools!

All 14 Calderdale secondary schools, including academies, plus the private schools, were sent an invitation in early October of the preceding year and 14 high schools were selected. There are usually five books chosen for each age group with reserves. It is essential that the authors are able to attend the Literary Lunch days – if they can't make it we go to the next novel on the reserve list. The chance to meet authors and talk to them about their novels is invaluable and generates huge enthusiasm for reading amongst the young people. Once the authors are booked the novels are ordered and are given out to the participating librarians or teachers. The school staff are responsible for choosing the young people to take part, who then read the books, discuss them and write reviews. Discover staff visit each of the schools during the discussion period. Coming along to the Literary Lunch at the Central Library gives the children a chance to vote for their favourite novel and meet two of the authors in a small workshop situation with the opportunity to ask questions of all the authors at a Q & A panel session at the end of the day. They are paired with another school and discuss the novels with them. Prize winning reviews receive copies of the novels and of course the winning book is announced. After a lengthy book signing session all depart happy and we start reading again for next year's awards!

Schools tell us that they appreciate the way CCBY provides a catalyst for an enriched reading culture in the school and reading groups set up for the awards can continue even when the school is not taking part in the Awards. We hear over and over that the experience gained of reading, discussing, and analysing novels with their peers enriches children's relationship with literature.

As well as the value it offers to the young people we hear so often from new authors that the chance to meet their reading public, often for the first time, is especially meaningful, as they feel encouraged that what they are doing is being appreciated by their intended audience.

What follows are the experiences of some the Calderdale High School Librarians who have been taking part in Calderdale Children's Book of the Year Awards, often for many years.

One school librarian explains

This is the only activity that the library targets specifically at more able students. We choose students from Year 8 by looking at their reading levels in English and cross-check with their library record. Usually we would know keen readers by Year 8 but if they tend to buy rather than borrow books, and keep their reading activity quiet, then the students may not have come to our attention previously.

Our meetings encourage the development of speaking and listening skills; groups tend to start off being very quiet and feeling self-conscious about expressing their views. By the time we get to the Awards they are much more self-assured and confident about speaking not just in front of each other but to a wider audience.

The scheme develops a holistic approach to reading and literacy as all aspects are discussed: we use the internet to find out more information about the authors and other books they may have written, we evaluate the author's websites, talk about and write book reviews, discuss the way books are published and how they are formatted and promoted differently in different countries.

Calderdale Children's Book of the Year Awards challenges students to read material they may never have chosen and helps to improve reading and literacy skills by students becoming familiar with a variety of writing styles.

Being involved in the Awards encourages library staff to participate in and arrange additional activities for students. Staff must anticipate and have a plan for each meeting in order to get the very best out of the process, but the rewards outweigh any organisational hiccups – the students taking part in the Awards continue as a reading group through school and last year saw our first Year 12 reading group as a result. Students and librarian tend to have a bond that lasts throughout their time at school and we find that students involved in these reading groups encourage other students to join the group in subsequent years, spread the word about reading and promote reading with their peers and within school. Our students will recommend books for the library to buy and will give their opinions on book suitability, such as age appropriateness.

Book of the Year at Brooksbank School
by Anne Ellis, Learning Resource Centre Manager

Students are chosen for their love of reading, some recommended by their English teachers and others regular borrowers in the LRC. Our Reading Groups run all year but the lucky students who are chosen to attend the Calderdale Children's Book of the Year Awards (CCBY) are from Years 8 and 9.

As we meet once per half term, roughly every six weeks, we like to start reading for the awards as soon as possible. We all read the same book at the same time, and to do this we buy extra copies to supplement the ones supplied by Discover. We also swap books with another High School to help reduce costs, agreeing on the order in which we will read before we begin.

At each Reading Group meeting we discuss the book we have read, whilst enjoying sandwiches and cake! Reviews are handed in and the next book and meeting date are distributed. This is a really good opportunity for the students to not only discuss the book we have been reading but to recommend other books that they have enjoyed.

The excitement builds as we get nearer the date of the awards and a visit to the school from a member of Discover to discuss what will happen on the day adds to this.

When asked what the students enjoyed the most they said, 'I have been introduced to books and authors that without Book of the Year I wouldn't have picked up', 'It was inspirational to hear from authors direct', 'I enjoyed the whole day especially the lunch'. The students loved talking to the authors and finding out how they wrote their stories and what inspired them.

Students who won prizes for their reviews were very pleased to be able to have their book prizes signed by the authors.

The only negative comment from students was that they were not able to attend when they reached Year 10!

The Brooksbank School have attended the awards from the day it began and hope that it will continue into the future. It is a wonderful opportunity for the students to celebrate reading for pleasure. Many thanks to all at Discover who make it such a fantastic event.

Calderdale Children's Book of the Year Award at The Crossley Heath Grammar School

by David Amdurer, Library Manager

The School Library (formerly the Learning Resource Centre), along with the English Department, run a number of literacy and reading initiatives throughout the year. The annual initiatives include author visits, an inter-House reading challenge, the Stan Lee Excelsior Awards and of course, the Calderdale Children's Book of the Year Awards (CCBY).

Since the shortlist of books for CCBY normally comes out early December, it means we can then use the list to spearhead a reading campaign based around the books for the rest of the year.

It's always an exciting time seeing the shortlist for the first time, checking which authors have made the list and which year group we think the list is being pitched at. Last year, the shortlist was a bit more senior which made it perfect for Year 9, whilst this year, it's going to be Year 8 students.

Although we can only take 8 to 10 students to the awards, we try and ensure that the group is composed of students with a range of abilities, from avid readers to those who rarely visit the library as well as students who would find participating in the awards a big boost to their self-confidence. The group is normally chosen by library staff with input from the English and SEN departments.

A display in the library of the shortlisted books with their plot summaries, along with publicity in the school newsletter, plus the students chosen to go to the awards telling their friends, all help to create an interest in the books by the entire lower school.

For CCBY, rather than have a structured reading group, we have found it best to let students read the books at their own pace, and in whatever order, with meetings every 6 to 8 weeks where students and staff can discuss how reading the shortlist is progressing, what everyone thinks of the books they have read to date and what reviews have been written.

By the time the awards themselves come around, students have read the books and are keen to meet the authors. Indeed, we almost had a riot last year when other students discovered that Cliff McNish was going to be there on the day – they all wanted to come.

That's the thing about the awards – something unexpected (in a good way), always turns up – from a favourite author of students, to an author who grew up at the same time as you and watched the same sci-fi (thanks Mike Lancaster and go

UFO), to an author who has just begun writing but scripted some of the biggest Hollywood comedies of the 1980s (William Osborne).

Long may the awards continue, and long may our students continue to enjoy and be excited by them.

Final words

And the final word comes from Chiamaka Chinweze, a student at North Halifax Grammar School:

> 'My first experience of the Calderdale Book of the Year Awards was in primary school and I enjoyed it so much, I did it at secondary school as well! The books were very interesting and diverse and I liked sharing my views on the book via reviews. The authors were friendly and gave great insight into what inspired them to write the books. Some of my reviews won and I got some free books which were all signed by the author. Overall, I really enjoyed the Calderdale Book of the Year Awards and found the experience thought-provoking and eventful.'

Case Study 5

The Red House Children's Book Award

Jo Huett

Librarian at Rossett School, Harrogate

Rossett School in Harrogate is involved in book testing for the Red House Children's Book Award (RHCBA). This is the only national book award voted for entirely by children. The nominated books are reviewed or 'tested' by children around the country and the most popular titles shortlisted. The shortlist consists of three categories; picture books for Younger Children, Books for Younger Readers and Books for Older Readers. Children can then vote for the winner of the three categories. The book with the most votes overall wins the Red House Children's Book Award.

The Red House Children's Book Award was founded in 1980 by Pat Thompson, a member of the Federation of Children's Book Groups. It was originally called The Children's Book Award until sponsorship from Red House books started in 2001. It's run on a voluntary basis by members of the Federation of Children's Book Groups which was set up to encourage children to read for pleasure. There are twelve local groups around the country who run testing groups but schools who don't have access to these groups can get involved in many other ways. We are members of the Harrogate Children's Book Group. The other groups are in Leeds, Plymouth, Reading, Oxted, Barrowby/Grantham, North London, Southampton, Birmingham and St Albans, a group in West Wales, and one in Dundee.

Publishers send copies of the books they want to nominate to all of the groups and the coordinators try to get as many children as possible to read each title. About 1,000 books are nominated in this way every year. The books must be newly published children's fiction, first published in the UK between 1st July and 30th June of the previous year. Together with about 30 other primary and secondary schools in the Harrogate and York area our students read and rate hundreds of books for the award. Our local coordinator receives eligible books from publishers and visits our school and others on a regular basis with boxes of books to loan out. We're very fortunate that our coordinator Marilyn Larner is passionate about books and her visits are eagerly anticipated. Despite being a volunteer she finds time to read lots of the books herself and is really good at tempting reluctant readers to try a book. The students borrow books in addition to their library loans and take a score sheet. When they have read the book they score the book and, if they wish, write comments. The score sheet is simple and quick to complete and the results are really useful to me; a high scoring book will make it onto my library purchases wish list! Students of all ages take part here, from Year Seven to Sixth Form. In between visits I swap books around the students, remind students to return them and publicise any upcoming visits by Twitter, messages at form time and posters around school. The schools encourage as many students as possible to get involved and at the end of this stage their votes are collected in and collated nationally.

The shortlist or Top Ten is announced and a new phase of reading starts. There are 10 books short-listed (based entirely on the reviews and scores collected in from the children) – usually four picture books, and three in each of the other two categories. The testing schools are able to buy subsidised sets of books in all the categories. I usually buy the Younger Readers and Older Readers sets and then get keen readers to commit to reading the three titles in one of the categories. They have to rank them in order of preference and these scores are also sent off by our coordinator. This year we also voted on the picture books; Marilyn attended our reading group meeting and brought the four picture books in for us to look at. She read them to read@rossett, our school book group (who thoroughly enjoyed being read to!) and they voted for their favourites. Voting for the picture books can tie into the curriculum or other groups as well. The picture books could also be used in Art lessons, with students studying for childcare qualifications, and with English Language students.

read@rossett members with Marilyn Larner
and some of the books for reviewing

It takes a little work to publicise the book testing and to manage the loans, keeping tabs on who has what, and I have also learnt that the more effort I put into publicising Marilyn's visits the better the attendance. The introduction of iPads in our school has meant that tweets about the Awards are very effective as they are seen by a large number of students. The benefits of being involved are immense. It gives our students access to a huge range of newly published titles, gives me ideas for new stock to purchase and adds to our promotion of reading for pleasure. The cost is very low as I just purchase the top ten titles for the older categories. When students return their books and scores to me in between visits it opens up lots of opportunities to discuss the books and what they liked and didn't like which helps forge positive relationships with regular library users and occasional users alike.

I asked some of the students involved why they enjoyed taking part; they all said they like it because it's voted for entirely by children so they know it is going to reflect their ideas of what makes a good read. They liked the extra choice of books it gave them in addition to the library stock which introduces them to new authors and genres. They liked having a completely free choice about which books to choose at the reviewing stage. Although they commit to reading three books in the Top Ten our students like this as they know these are the most popular with their age group so they know that they will be enjoyable. They liked having a mixture of established, well known authors as well as authors they might not have heard about before. The simple voting system also got the thumbs up. The students enjoy getting involved as they don't need to write a long review in the testing process – they can just score a book and write some brief comments if they wish.

> 'I love using Red House Book Testing because it offers a variety of books which I may or may not have even considered reading, it also allows students to explore new authors who they may not have heard of. This has benefitted me because I don't always have time to go looking for new books. I would recommend this to anyone.'
> —Sixth Form student

> 'The Red House book testing helped me to read books I wouldn't usually read anyway and it gave me access to a wider range of books but it also it allowed me to talk with people about books I read that read similar things to me.'
> —Year 10 student

I like the fact that I can incorporate the reviewing and voting into my reading group activities but it's not restricted to that, as I run the testing at lunchtimes as well and involve lots of other students. The number of students involved varies from year to year and fluctuates during the year too, depending on students' other school activities, exams etc. and also depends on how many books are available for testing as the books get circulated round the other schools involved. We keep it very open and if a student happens to come along when the book swapping is going on and shows interest it's a chance to engage them and get them involved. When I publicise a book testing session it is open to all ages and abilities and some students dip in and out as it suits them. Publicity about the book testing also raises the profile of reading, literacy and the Resource Centre around school, and contributes to our whole school reading culture. A book testing session is an 'event' and adds variety to what the Resource Centre offers and gives an additional opportunity to enthuse students about reading for pleasure.

There are some fantastic resources on the Red House Book Award website, including competitions and teacher/librarian resources. There is a certificate of achievement for taking part which is great for assemblies or tutor time. Red House also publishes a really useful leaflet with their Pick of the Year, which lists the fifty most popular books including the Top Ten. This is available on the website along with Pick of the Year from previous years. I've given copies to parents at Open Days and Parents Evening when they have asked for reading suggestions, along with the Resource Centre book lists.

If schools don't have access to a testing group nearby they can still get involved by voting for the Top Ten as votes can be cast as individuals or as school groups. If running it as a school group the posters, certificates and bookmarks on the website would be very useful and a lot of the benefits such as raising the library profile, promoting literacy and encouraging reading would still be achieved for a relatively low cost.

Last year we were lucky enough to be invited to attend the Red House Children's Book Awards Ceremony. It takes place every year in February as part of the Imagine Children's Festival at London's Southbank. All the testing groups are offered complimentary tickets for a small number of people to attend and the local coordinator decides who to invite from the schools and families involved in the local group.

Our RHCBA coordinator Marilyn, a Rossett School English teacher, and I took four of our students to London for the day. I selected students who had been actively involved in both stages of the reviewing and voting and they had all read the Top Ten. Our students met the authors and collected lots of autographs. We sat with author Suzanne LaFleur at the celebratory lunch and then attended the ceremony where our students went up on stage with Patrick Ness and presented the award for the Older Readers category to Sophie McKenzie for her book *The Medusa Project; Hit Squad*. All the authors and illustrators receive a wonderfully presented portfolio of children's work (consisting of children's letters and pictures) and the category winners each receive an engraved silver bookmark. The overall winner is awarded a trophy to display for the year and a silver acorn to keep. It was a very long but very exciting day and inspiring to hear the authors talk about how they had become writers.

Even if a school isn't linked to a book group it's still possible to attend the Award Ceremony and it's very enjoyable. Tickets are available from the Federation of Children's Book Groups and sometimes they are offered as competition prizes on the Red House Book Children's Book Award website.

Rossett School students onstage with the Overall Winners Andrew Weale and Lee Cornish for Spooky Spooky House

The English teacher who accompanied us said:

'Last year I was involved in our Red House book testing group's trip to London, and it was completely brilliant. We were lucky enough to attend the prize giving ceremony where our students met many of the prize winning authors and illustrators in person. The feedback for the authors is so worthwhile, since it all comes from their readers, and the benefits for the children involved are numerous. Besides improving their literacy skills, the testing groups also offer students a chance to meet other book lovers and make friends while doing something they really enjoy. Red House reviewing is something we are really fortunate to be involved with and being at the awards ceremony was a wonderful and inspiring experience, for the children – and for me!'

*Imogen meeting the illustrator of 'The World of Norm' books,
Donough O'Malley*

I know how much the other school librarians in the area value being involved in this award; recently the future of Harrogate Children's Book Group was in doubt as the previous Chair announced she wanted to step down. If the group had folded the local schools would not have been able to continue testing for the RHCBA so a group of librarians from schools involved got together to form a new committee, a sign of their willingness and commitment to promoting reading in this way.

For more information on the Red House Children's Book Award and to see the available resources visit their website www.redhousechildrensbookaward.co.uk.

To find out more about the Federation of Children's Book Groups and see if there is a group near you, visit www.fcbg.org.uk.

Case Study 6

Leeds Book Awards

Pauline Thresh BA (Hons) MCLIP

Manager of the Leeds School Library Service

The Leeds Book Awards (LBA) are run annually by Leeds School Library Service (SLS) and public libraries. They have developed to become a fantastic opportunity for children and young people (CYP) to take part and vote for the best books published in the categories 9–11, 11–14 and 14–16.

Brief introduction to the Awards

The Leeds Book Awards have been running now for seven years. Although we were committed to the Carnegie and Greenaway Awards, we wanted to create our own Book Award scheme to give CYP a greater voice and influence. Through the LBA, CYP can suggest titles for consideration and their votes decide the winners.

Leeds is a child friendly city, and we always appreciate and value young people's contributions and views on the work that is being undertaken by our libraries.

We love being able to give young people a voice to say how they feel about the shortlisted books. We also have a dedicated website where young people can post their own reviews about the books, and last year we received over 1,000 reviews.

We listen to evaluations and this helps us to develop year on year – even if that means more work, which it usually does!

School participation has grown enormously over the life of the Awards. We started with 25 schools taking part, which has grown this year to 78 schools.

Young people don't have to be members of school book groups to take part in the Awards – anyone can borrow the shortlisted books through their local library, post reviews on the website and vote for their favourite by filling out a form at the library.

What type of books do we want to highlight for the Awards?

The books on our shortlists must have been published within the last 12 months. They must be standalone reads, so no series fiction or sequels, although the first book in a new series is fine.

We look for riveting reads – titles that young people will find thoroughly enjoyable and engaging and will want to recommend to all their friends.

How we manage the Awards

The Awards are planned by a 12-member LBA project group, part of the CYP project team for libraries. It is led by the SLS Manager, with the Young People's Librarian for Leeds, and library staff at all levels as part of the team.

The aim of the group is to successfully deliver LBA with increased school participation and to have a positive influence on Children's Services.

The project groups' objectives are to:

- Plan deliver and evaluate LBA
- Give CYP an opportunity to enjoy and share their opinions on a range of exciting contemporary books
- Develop wider involvement with public libraries
- Improve links with schools including those not previously involved
- Celebrate success and communicate widely
- Explore ways to increase the profile of the Awards to ensure that it maintains prominence nationally as well as locally.

Planning the LBA as a project group gives library staff the opportunity to work with colleagues from different parts of the service that they would not normally have the chance to do, whilst developing their skills, and boosting knowledge and confidence in children's books. They are also involved in the planning of one of the largest events in the library calendar.

Engaging staff at all levels ensures that the LBA is promoted to all CYP in the city, whether in the library or a school group.

How it works

The LBA runs throughout the year.

The project group has devised a very comprehensive timeline which outlines on a monthly basis, what has to be done, when and by whom.

- May - The call for long list nominations goes out, with a deadline of early November. Nominations come from the children and young people themselves, school librarians, teachers and library staff.

- September – A call for publisher submissions goes out. Publishers can submit up to 2 titles per category for consideration.

- September to November, schools register for the Awards. There is a registration fee – the price includes a set of books, training where appropriate, access to the website and invitation to Awards Ceremony.

- November, the shortlist is announced by the team.

- January – books and publicity are distributed to school groups and libraries.

- January – informal training session for teachers new to the Awards, where they can network with other LBA groups, and their local librarian sharing ideas and experiences, thus ensuring no-one feels isolated. For librarians it is an opportunity to form links and networks from which come many contacts for future working.

- January to April the CYP are reading, sharing, discussing and reviewing the shortlist. Peer recommendation is vitally important.

- Anyone can take part, not necessarily limited to Leeds, and it's so exciting to share the reviews on the site. The CYP love it, as they have been given a voice and can express themselves freely. Grammar is not corrected, only inappropriate language or plot spoilers are prohibited.

The impact of the Awards on the CYP can be seen in the reviews below:

Slated (by Teri Terry)

'I found the book hard to understand at the beginning and looking at the cover and reading the first few chapters, I had decided to my self that I was not going to like this book. I told my friend, who was also reading Slated that it is totally rubbish. I take that back. Because now I have learnt a valuable lesson, not to judge a book by its cover and to give it a chance. I had never read a book like Slated before as I am not keen on futuristic novels, but reading Slated has taught me to try new things, and I rather enjoyed the book.'

- **April** – CYP across the city vote for their favourite read, thus having total influence on the winning book.
- **May** – Two separate events are then held in May, one for primary and one for high schools.

The authors and schools are invited to hear the announcement of the winner, and to have the exciting opportunity to meet each other.

There is participation from the young people at both events. In response to evaluations from previous events we have worked out what really works well for young people at the events.

For the 9–11 event schools give presentations about the shortlisted books – the presentations are fun and quirky and are always a big hit both with the audience and the authors in attendance.

For the high school event for the 11–14 and 14–16 categories what works best is a more informal discussion format with the authors plus the opportunity for 'Q & A' from the young people. School groups 'adopt' an author for the afternoon – they meet, greet and look after an author before the event begins. This gives them a chance to ask lots of questions as well as making the author feel welcomed and at ease before the proceedings. This works really well, and the impact of the events is beyond measure.

Where we are now?

The Awards are CYP led. The shortlist can be titles suggested by them, read by them, reviewed and voted for. The result is not decided by adults or library staff.

Here's a lovely message from Rachel Billington our 9–11 winner in 2013:

'I can't tell you how much I enjoyed the Leeds Book Awards. It was not just that Poppy's Hero won, although that was very very exciting, but that the whole morning was so heartening… it was an enormous feat to get together so many schools in one place and inspire such a positive and happy atmosphere… The next day I looked at the email reviews for all the books and was even more impressed – particularly by the girl who gave Poppy's Hero four rather than five stars because 'every book can be improved' or something similar. Quite right.'

Here are some of the primary children's comments from the 2013 ceremony:

'I liked having the chance to meet the authors.'

'Everything was great'!

'I liked the presentations best because people can show what they found out from the book.'

'It was brilliant.'

The high school ceremony was at Leeds Civic Hall on Thursday 23 May 2013. 200 young people attended and they met 10 of the 12 shortlisted authors. Feedback from the high school event revealed that the YP enjoyed meeting the authors the most, followed by having a book signing opportunity.

Involvement in the Book Awards generates a huge buzz around the school, demonstrating a real excitement for reading and there is a kudos attached to being involved for the young people. One only has to experience the Award days to see the excitement on the children and young people's faces. It really is the best day in the library/SLS calendar. The biggest problem is booking appropriate venues as so many schools taking part also want to attend the ceremony.

For the young people involved it is a very sociable activity and one in which they can join together with others – sharing reviews on the website and rooting for their particular favourites. It gives them the confidence to express their views and they feel that what they think really matters.

Future plans

We are continually looking for ways to develop the Awards and want to expand our marketing strategy. We are also looking at live streaming possibilities to enable involvement on the day for schools that cannot physically be present at the Award ceremony. A social media presence via Twitter is also being developed.

We are now working with the British Comic Awards as they develop their Young People's Category and this year eleven schools and one public library group from Leeds have taken part in the British Comic Awards. This enables us to offer more reading opportunities to a more diverse audience: www.britishcomicawards.com.

One of our high school librarians describes their involvement in this way:

The Comic Book Award especially appeals to students who find traditional narratives difficult to access. I often find that students who are in lower English sets want to participate in the comic awards.

One student told me 'I never used to read until I did this. It got me into reading'. Many students love comic books but somehow feel that reading them isn't viewed as 'proper reading' by their teachers. I believe that the comic book award plays a valuable role in changing these perceptions and in recognising the value of comic books in developing reading skills and promoting reading for pleasure.

Pupils from Pudsey Southroyd Primary School with Rachel Billington after performing their drama review of her book in 2013.

Impact

The parent of a Year 9 student who took part in 2011 contacted us to say:

'I just wanted to thank everyone involved for organising the Book Awards – my daughter came home yesterday glowing, more enthusiastic and happy than school has ever made her.

'She'd chatted with several authors, even stood up and addressed the entire assembly on 'The Radleys'. She's usually reluctant to put herself forward at all, but said 'It was safe – everyone there was a nerd' (she meant that in a good way!). A really positive experience.'

To show the impact and kudos amongst the CYP taking in part, one primary teacher commented:

'The Book Awards in general has been a pleasure to be involved in as ever, and I'm particularly pleased that it's not just the book group who are enjoying the books. The copies we received have now gone into Year 5 and Year 6 class libraries and the buzz generated by the book group has made them extremely popular, so many more children are now discovering some brilliant new authors!'

Greenaway Shadowing: The Danum Academy Experience

Lynne Coppendale, BA(Hons), PGDipIS, MCLIP
Librarian at Danum Academy, Doncaster

Introduction

The Kate Greenaway Medal was established in 1955, for distinguished illustration in a book for children. It is named after the popular 19th century artist known for her fine children's illustrations and designs (www.carnegiegreenaway.org.uk/greenaway). Aware of both the Carnegie and the Greenaway shadowing schemes since qualifying and taking up my first professional post in a school back in 1997, it was not until moving to Danum Academy that shadowing Greenaway seemed a possibility. Prior to this, as a secondary school librarian, I had made the mistaken assumption that Greenaway was for primary children, or younger.

Background

Doncaster had a thriving school librarians' group and it was one I joined immediately I took up employment at Danum Academy, in July 2000. Led by Trevor Finch it was a hive of activity and sharing of best practice, and it was at one of these meetings that Jane Flynn, then KS3 Librarian at Hall Cross (now Librarian of Hall Cross Academy), led a training session for us all using her school's participation in Greenaway shadowing as an exemplar. At this time Jane's school collaborated with her Art Department and three feeder schools, organising myriad different art activities based on the Greenaway shortlist. It was felt to be an invaluable introduction for the younger students to the 'Big School', and a perfect transition project that included staff from both schools and students of all ages.

Danum Begins

Taking this idea on board I organised to do just such a project alongside a member of our Art Department and also included the ideas, organisation and session leading skills of Sixth Form art students. Unfortunately time has marched on, and the exact titles on the shortlist of this first year of shadowing for us escape me, however the art work included pottery, drawing, mask-making, a large collage, different styles of painting and involved lots of gluing, sticking and using different materials. All the activities were devised and led by Sixth Formers under the guidance of the art teacher with whom I was working. We had two of our six primaries take part this first year, one with KS1 students and the other with top end KS2. I took on the organising details of any trips out to the schools and their return visits to take part in the artwork. It is the organisational element which I retain to this day, behind the scenes smoothing the path of the teachers' and students' undertakings.

Outcomes

Specific outcomes were set. The students were expected to read, or have read to them, all the books on the shortlist. Danum Academy purchased three sets of the shortlist, one for the Art Department, one for the Library and the third remained with me and was taken to all schools as I visited them.

Reviews are expected from participants and, as one may expect, I do the moderation and run any online groups. The evolution of our shadowing meant some schools asked me to run weekly reading groups, others to visit for an award introduction (using a prepared PowerPoint by Chris Fitt,[1] which I update annually and use to this day), once during the process and as host of the joint Finale. At our busiest I have run seven of these groups, when one year we had all six of our partner primaries taking part. Guidance is given to all students to help them complete their reviews, including sentence starter reviews, which are also used in my secondary reading group (the Final Chapter) to help students.

Danum Continues

As primary staff members move on, participation from the primary schools varies and not all now take part. Danum's partner primaries have tended to enjoy Greenaway Shadowing as a Transition project with their Year 5 or, more commonly, Year 6 students and for some I attended weekly and ran reading groups, whereas for others I just popped in twice and then organised the Finale event. A particularly popular activity was arranging for each primary group to attend a 'Picbits' event, organised by Chris Fitt, within their local branch library. This involved the students matching small parts of pictures which were displayed around the libraries, to the book from which they originated. It is incredibly popular and the students never failed to amaze with their knowledge of the artwork and their success in matching. Small prizes were provided either by Chris, the library or me, or more often a combination thereof. More recently, work

---

[1] Children's Reading 'Enthuser', Freelance librarian and former Doncaster Libraries Children's Librarian.

prepared by Year 6 shadowers has included animation and music composition, plays, dances, re-written endings and comic strips. All my participants celebrated in a joining together Finale hosted by me at our school, or a suitable more central venue, at which their artwork was displayed and the Greenaway results were announced. This is another task I took on, ensuring each student's vote was counted and then announced as an individual school result, a Danum Pyramid result and then, of course, the 'actual' genuine result. I made sure to always photograph events, indeed a few have been video'd, to ensure the students' reactions were captured, as very rarely do they agree with the adult judges' choices! I have been unable to get into our primaries to run such groups for the last three years, and am unsure whether I could give as much time as I have in previous years due to in-house changes to Danum's libraries, but I still try every year.

This does not mean Danum's participation has decreased however. Far from it – as the primaries dropped out, Danum's staff took up the reins!

For the past two years every single Year 7 student, in addition to the Lower School Library's reading group, Final Chapter, has taken part in the shadowing. Danum had a specific scheme entitled LEAP, which meant that outside of core subject areas students identified as academically in need of assistance, and possibly needing help transitioning to secondary school, were placed in classes with which they remained for the majority of the school day. These students took on Greenaway shadowing as a Literacy project through which they enhanced their reading, increased their enjoyment of books and grew in confidence. As with the primary schools, reviews and art/writing projects were produced and we held an in-house special assembly to present work and reveal the results of voting. This scheme began five years ago and was replicated two years later with our Non-LEAP students within their humanities (individual subjects combined and called Opening Minds) classes. In addition to reviews this group produced their own books, which were displayed in a Fayre at the end of the project and which were judged and given prizes. All Year 7 students therefore participated in some way and thoroughly enjoyed themselves.

Moderating the Greenaway Shadowing groups is hard work for me, but often I was team-teaching the classes. Having introduced the scheme at the start, this meant I then had time during those classes to moderate, and this also permitted an informal competition between classes as I pointed out whether LEAP were beating Opening Minds or vice versa! An unintended, but welcome, outcome was the increase in student numbers coming to the library, being happy to talk to and ask questions of the staff and feeling ownership of what is their resource.

Park Primary 2009. Sandringham Primary Picbits Quiz in local library.

Finale

The final event has long been key to Doncaster Schools' shadowing schemes and we have joined together as secondary schools to celebrate the end of the Carnegie Medal for as long as I can remember. This was duplicated for Greenaway as soon as at least two of us were shadowing and is something I continue to do.

Resources

There will be some financial outlay to the project. It may be that your library capitation can cover costs, or you can request support from your schools' Literacy pot, or perhaps your Art Department may provide some materials and get involved. Purchasing the short list is vital, but how many sets of the shortlist depends upon funding available and your particular needs. Calculating the time you can realistically give to each participating group is important, as overextending oneself means no-one gets the best. When organising such a project, partnership working is advised with a clear delineation of the roles. Everything else depends upon your budget and the activities you wish to do. Trips out to join with other school groups for meetings or events will necessitate the appropriate risk assessment and, potentially, trip fees if you need to charge your students for travel.

Limitations

There is one limitation only — your imagination! As we always tell our students, reading truly engages the brain and opens up our experiences, not least from the wonderfully rich books that make the Greenaway shortlist. If you do not automatically receive a copy of your whole school development plan, then ask for a copy (Office Manager, Head Teacher's PA, Director of Business, whoever is appropriate in your school structure). Comb through this to see which key areas of development Greenaway Shadowing can meet. It is much easier to encourage participation in an extra-curricular project if the people whom you are targeting can see clearly the benefits being met in terms of schemes of work. If you feel able, provide lesson plans for each activity you intend to offer, offer a few and let participants pick and choose.

Greenaway Shadowing has long been an invaluable tool with which to engage our Partner Primary students as a transition project, as well as our less able students and those for whom the written word format of reading is not a preferred option. Evidence of work produced is plentiful and meets many learning targets. Artwork, Design, Drama and such subjects are incredibly SEN-friendly and can, in many ways, require little or no lone reading. In our case, to require all our students to individually read the books is impractical and something we only ever ask as a voluntary activity by students when a book is too long to read aloud to the class. Reading aloud is a popular and tranquil time for our students; they are engaged in the story not passively, as one may think, but through listening and active engagement in a relaxed setting. The rendition of Ed Vere's 'Banana' by Mr Gill of Plover Primary is one which is retained in memory by everyone who ever heard it and was oft demanded for many years after the book appeared on the shortlist.

Through Greenaway our students have become active, involved readers, keen critics and able library users. How we will shadow this academic year is yet to be decided, but shadow we will.

Town Field Primary at our first ever Finale est. 2003

Case Study 8

The James Reckitt Hull Children's Book Award

Christine Hill

Principal Librarian, Hull Libraries

Introduction

The first Hull Children's Book Award took place in 2007 with seven primary schools and seven secondary schools. Over the years the award has grown and evolved into a prestigious event with forty primaries and ten secondary schools taking part more recently, and with each year the participation increases.

Before the book award in Hull some Carnegie Greenaway shadowing had taken place, but in 2007 it was felt that the time was right to develop an award that would better meet the needs of the children in Hull and, after some consultation, it was decided to deliver the award at two levels – Key Stage 2 and Key Stage 3.

The outcomes for the award were set at the beginning and over the last seven years have formulated the way in which the award is now run. The systems and processes of the award have evolved, but the overall aims and objectives first envisaged remain the same.

The award aims to:

- foster a love of reading for pleasure for young people
- introduce them to new authors and new reading choices, thus extending their reading skills
- encourage reading outside of the national curriculum - all too often pupils are given sections of books to read for academic purposes but never a whole one, so the award encourages them to read whole books stretching their reading abilities
- facilitate discussion with both peers and adults, so improving speaking and listening skills
- encourage reading in a non-school environment
- support and inspire family reading

- raise self-esteem amongst pupils via the exclusivity of the award
- raise the profile of the library service encouraging non-members to join.

It was initially agreed that each school would decide how best to operate the book award within their own schools, and therefore different methods of selecting pupils to take part have been used by the teaching staff and school librarians. These are identified as follows:

- All children in the school are informed about the award and then asked to volunteer to take part
- A class or year group is pre-selected by the teaching staff and they are then asked who would like to volunteer
- Teaching staff select a whole class and the books are then read as a 'class read'. The reading group for the award is then made up of the most avid readers
- Children are selected according to their ability by the teaching staff, i.e. 'gifted and talented'
- Children selected are the most enthusiastic and who it is felt would benefit most from being involved.

However they are selected, all of the children involved feel a sense of exclusivity by participating in the book award. They are either part of a regular lunchtime reading group where the books are discussed with teaching or library staff, some read the books as home readers and in one school the children who volunteered to take part organised their own reading schedule, so giving them total ownership.

I think it is true to say that however the children are selected, they all enjoy taking part and attending the voting day.

Timeline for the award

- From January to December, suitable books that are published during this time are placed on a long list,[2] these are read and evaluated by our team of librarians, school staff and volunteers, each book is then given a score, and all this information is sent to the School Library Service for staff to collate.

---

2   The suitable books for the award are chosen by the librarians and SLS manager choosing from the new stock received. Suitable means:
   • within the age range / ability KS2 / KS3
   • books should not be part of a series unless it is the first one
   • new authors are always considered, so we don't always go for the popular names.

- From September to November the School Library Service invites the schools to participate and register their interest to take part in the award.

- A meeting is arranged in December and a shortlist of five books for each Key Stage is agreed. This is negotiated by those who have been reading and evaluating throughout the year. The evaluations and scoring for each book is discussed at this meeting and the shortlist is created.

- Contact is then made with the shortlisted authors and their publishers.

- In January our shortlisted titles are delivered to all the participating schools. It is then up to the schools to decide how they develop it in their school setting. This is where the learning, encouragement and good work takes place.

- Currently, voting takes place in May for KS3, secondary schools and in June for KS2, primary schools.

Voting day KS2 2013 in Hull City Hall

Book Award Profiles

Here are two profiles from secondary school librarians who have both been part of the award since the beginning.

Profile A

We have done the Book Award in School every year since it began. We find that it gives the Library a positive focus during the Spring Term.

The Book Award has grown over the years and now with the added bonus of author visits is a major part of the library calendar in school. We are developing an extensive reading culture at Kelvin Hall with the Accelerated Reader programme and the Book Award is a wonderful extension of this work.

I generally hand pick the students that I think are capable of reading all the nominated titles. A class group would probably work if it was a top set, but if the students were in a class of mixed ability, you would probably struggle to get all students to read all the books.

The books generally vary in difficulty, which is to be expected, so you do need to have students who enjoy reading enough to be motivated to take up the challenge. The success of the voting day totally relies on the students having read all the titles. Staff involved also need to be committed to reading the nominated titles.

Reading the titles from differing genres is a challenge for all students but can only benefit their overall reading ability and extend their future reading choices. Just the fact that they are talking regularly about the books they are reading with their peers can only be a positive thing.

We try and meet regularly with the reading group to keep everyone motivated; I also always have a colour coded spread sheet so that I can closely monitor their reading.

I always tell the students at the beginning of the process that they have to read all titles or they will not be able go on the voting day. I also ask the students to fill in a review form and hand it back to me so that I know that each book has been read. This is useful, on the day, to hand back to the students as a reminder for them of the detail in each book.

This year at Kelvin Hall we are going to tie the Book Award in with School Report. We are going to do this in house using the TV broadcast system and green screen we have on site. We also have access to easy speak microphones and cameras.

The students will be off timetable for the day, some will write newspaper articles, others will act as television reporters, interviewing each other on the books they have read. We will hopefully be able to televise the results on the big screens we have in and around the school building.

Paula Suddards (Librarian, Kelvin Hall School, Hull)

Profile B

Winifred Holtby Academy has taken part in the Hull Children's Book Awards since the first year it was organised. Prior to that, we used to do the Carnegie Book Award.

I have always advertised it to any students who are interested. This may include students who are of a lower reading age than that of the books and, because of this, they do not always manage to read all of the five books but I would never discourage anyone from trying.

Our school uses Accelerated Reader, and every student in year 7-9 has to read an Accelerated Reader book. It therefore helps if the books that are chosen for the book award have AR quizzes.

However, the benefits of students reading the book award titles, as librarians know, are many, such as reading genres that they would not otherwise read, discovering new authors, and stretching their imaginations, but this is hard to evidence in a school without data.

Over the years that our school has taken part, I have not seen a decrease in enthusiasm for taking part, but a definite struggle by the students to complete all of the five books due to a lack of reading ability. Our average reading age in KS3 is about 9–10 years, and many students have a reading age much lower than this.

The demands on students' time are much more intense than they were, with schools doing early entry exams. Everything is about data, and that is why titles that have Accelerated Reader quizzes are favoured because then reading for pleasure can be evidenced in terms of improvement.

I believe that if 35 students start off reading but only manage one or two books, then these are two books that they might not have thought of reading, two books that might change their opinion of an author or a genre. The ones who do persevere and manage to read 4 to 5 books are the only ones that I would allow to go to the Book Award, because then they can fully contribute to the discussion. Schools should not allow students to attend unless they read at least 4 books.

Benefits include: group discussion, meeting the authors, and putting a face to a name, reading a different genre, feeling part of a wider reading community, confidence to debate a book and give opinions.

Some students, who have taken part in Year 7, continue to take part each year. I take a photograph each year and have a display from 2008 onwards in the LRC. This causes great amusements when students can look back at how they have changed from when they were in Year 7, or they recognise a student who left last year. It is also useful to see which books were nominated in a particular year. There is a buzz around the Library at this time and the students who are reading talk about the books, and make new friendship groups. Having the authors visit the schools in the lead up to the book awards keeps the momentum going.

Jean Oliver, Learning Resource Manager, Winifred Holtby Academy, Hull

One primary school has developed the participation and the skills of its pupils by using the award as part of a media group. They came to the award last year with cameras and filmed some of the process and interviewed children from other schools.

As organisers we have also engaged with a local partner, 'Creative Partnerships', which has filmed some of the past voting days and encouraged children to take part in interviewing each other about their reading and what they think to the books shortlisted. This is very inspiring and gives the young people confidence and aspiration to try something new.

Finance and marketing

To operate a book award is not without cost however it is delivered. In 2007 funding for the award in Hull was sought and gained from a number of sources. These included the local area youth network teams and a number of small businesses, as well as support from the city council public and school library service, with in-kind support for staff time. In the early days too only the winning author was invited to an award ceremony.

Finance is required for the following:

- To purchase enough shortlisted books – we send approximately five copies of each shortlisted title into every school taking part
- To hire spaces for each voting day – as the award grows big enough spaces are harder to find
- Voting day is from 10:00 to 15:00 so we have always provided lunch
- Promotional material, bookmarks with shortlisted titles, pull ups
- Every child receives a 'goody bag' to take home containing stationery e.g. note pad and pencil as well as a new book for each child to keep
- Author visits
- Prize for winning author.

Today all five shortlisted authors from each key stage are invited to deliver class sessions in school beforehand and all are invited to the voting day where the winner is announced and the prize presented to the winning author. This has been one of the ways the award has evolved and it delivers more impact for the children. To have the author available to tell them about their book and answer questions is invaluable and is very inspirational for the young people, and the authors who have participated in this way have all found it to be very enjoyable and extremely rewarding.

We are very fortunate in Hull to have the James Reckitt Library Trust which now funds the award each year, hence the name of the award.

The James Reckitt Library Trust was established as an independent charitable trust in 1892 by Sir James Reckitt (1833–1924), the pioneering industrialist and philanthropist. Originally intended to support the James Reckitt Library in east Hull, it now helps to develop public library provision throughout the City. The projects and activities which it funds are designed to stimulate a love of reading and learning, particularly among children and young people, to encourage those who might not normally use public library services to do so, and to raise awareness of what modern public libraries can offer.

To relay the story of Sir James Reckitt and his involvement in the instigation of public libraries in Hull, a book about his life and times has been published and is given to each child who participates (Harper, Victoria. *The Life and Times of Sir James Reckitt*. Hull: Kingston Press).

Comments

There are a number of things that make the award rewarding, but the main thing is the young people who take part and what they get from participating. They always enjoy the voting day and one of the things they really appreciate is the contact with students from other schools.

The young people love reading the books and having discussions about them, you really have to take part to fully understand the 'buzz' around the room, and it's all about reading – fantastic!

The following are just a few of the positive comments we have received from the young people who have taken part in previous years:

'I enjoyed reading books I wouldn't normally choose'

'The range of books was amazing'

'friendly atmosphere and a good day'

'It's amazing'

'Getting a wider perspective on different books'

'Finding out about others opinions'

'The chance to read more varied books that I wouldn't normally read'

'It was really good because you get to make new friends'.

We also receive positive comments from the visiting authors who have expressed how well they feel the award is run, and that they know exactly what is expected of them on the day.

I believe the award is achieving great success and delivering everything it intended when it first began, this is because of the continuous evaluation and willingness to improve.

In 2017 Hull is the City of Culture, and the James Reckitt Hull Children's Book Award will also celebrate its 10th Anniversary… some very big celebrations are being planned in Hull!

For more information about the James Reckitt Hull Children's Book Award please contact: Christine.hill@hullcc.gov.uk or hullschools.library@hullcc.gov.uk.

Case Study 9

The Education Ossett Community Trust (OECT)/SLS Wakefield Riveting Reads Book Award

Monica O'Neill

LRC Co-ordinator at Ossett Academy & Sixth Form College

Lesley Marshall

Senior Cultural Officer, Wakefield Schools Library Service (SLS)

Background

Reading for pleasure is such a vital activity for children of all ages to pursue and the benefits of it have been well documented over the last 10 years. Ossett is a historic market town with a population of over 21,000 located in Wakefield with 11 schools (consisting of education model of Infant, Primary and Secondary Schools).

As the Learning Resources Centre's Co-ordinator for Ossett Academy I felt that although we were shadowing our neighbouring Borough's Book Award I wasn't really tackling the bigger issue locally. How could I engage more children *in our local community* to read and develop a love of reading for pleasure? I wanted to engage our Primary colleagues and as a team work together to embed a culture of reading into our children's psyche across the town.

I feel what was really needed is to create an *Ossett Community of Readers!* allowing all pupils, from all schools in the town, to share their views and opinions on books. This would provide both reluctant and committed readers the opportunity to engage with some of the best new fiction titles on the market through a unique partnership arrangement with the Schools' Library Service in Wakefield.

Furthermore, I wanted students to engage with new authors that they would not necessarily have read before and evaluate and review books for their peers, making it a truly student-led Book Award!

Additionally, the Book Award concept provided a great opportunity to run a unique transition project with our feeder primary schools. This would make the transition process for students between primary and secondary education less daunting and a smooth positive experience through our Learning Resources Centre (LRC).

As part of the shortlist process one of the aims was that primary school students were able to visit the Academy's LRC and get to know the LRC staff, work with current Ossett Academy students and return back to school as reading role models for their school. Students would be able to feed back their positive experiences of both the Awards and the Academy.

EOCT and Getting the Awards off the Ground in 2011

The Education Ossett Community Trust (EOCT) consists of 9 out of the 11 schools in Ossett.

- South Ossett Infants School
- Dimple Well Infants School
- Southdale
- Towngate
- Flushdyke
- Holy Trinty
- Gawthorpe
- Highfield
- Ossett Academy & Sixth Form

However, the Book Award has always been about inclusion, inclusion, inclusion. Therefore, the remaining two primary schools, namely St Ignatius and South Parade School in Ossett, also participate in this Book Award, which means all the schools in Ossett participate.

Along with the Head's approval I had to pitch the Book Award concept to all the Trust School Heads and the School Library Service, Wakefield (our partners). Although professionally daunting, the pitch went extremely well with a 100% take up at the meeting. The headteachers were extremely enthusiastic, supportive and had some fantastic ideas to contribute too.

Lesley Marshall from the School Library Service in Wakefield continues describing our journey. *'We jumped at the chance, as we'd been discussing for a while how a small SLS team like ours could get involved in this area.'*

At an initial meeting, we spoke about the kind of award we wanted and who to involve. We quickly decided that we wanted the students at all Ossett schools (in the Trust and the Ossett pyramid) to choose the shortlists and winner and to be excited about their choices. We chose the name 'EOCT/SLS Wakefield Riveting

Reads Book Award' and students were to choose the most exciting, gripping, thrilling book they had read, which has been published in paperback the previous year. We also decided that we'd like a Book Club Co-ordinator in each school (11 schools in all) to run a Year 5/6 book group, which would meet weekly and act as reading ambassadors in their school. SLS staff were allocated specific schools to support these groups and provide books.

Resources

SLS provides a box of resources in September for each participating group. The resources are selected throughout the year ready for the following year, so the process never stops. Each school receives about 30 books, which means a lot of new stock is going into a few schools initially, but it comes back into SLS at the end of the year to benefit all our schools.

Additionally, in the Summer Term all students are asked to feed their book recommendations into the scheme. These recommendations can then be added to boxes prior to distribution if they meet the criteria.

Lesley states *'the students are really excited when they receive their new books and then the fun starts, as they read, share, discuss and take part in lots of book-related activities at their school.'*

As a Team (SLS, all the Book Club Co-ordinators and myself), initially came up with lots of reading activities and ideas, which we share through Ossett Academy's VTLE. All parties have access to this knowledge portal, which provides advice, guidance, Book Club related activities and templates, key dates for the diary, photos of previous events etc, basically, everything schools need to shadow the Awards.

Furthermore, we have regular termly meetings with all Book Club Co-ordinators and all parties involved at the Academy. This is to ensure everyone involved is supported and it allows for a sharing of knowledge, experience and good practice between schools, which enables all schools to participate and have a unique role in the Book Awards.

Lesley goes on to state that *'Initially, the SLS staff undertook quite a few reading group sessions, but as Book Club Co-ordinators have grown in confidence and experience, this role has lessened over the years.'*

The public library also plays their part in the shadowing process by promoting the Awards at Ossett Library and loaning books so that students can recommend titles for the long list. The public library staff are also invited to the Awards Ceremony.

Another Award!

As the EOCT/SLS, Wakefield Book Riveting Reads Book Awards was predominately targeted at Key Stage 2 along with consultation with our Infant Schools, we decided as a team to run a second Award, the EOCT/SLS Wakefield Picture Book Awards. Again, using the School Library Service, Wakefield's resources and experienced staff, recruiting new Key Stage 1 Book Club Co-ordinators from each school and support from our EOCT Co-ordinator, this second Award has taken off! A further two schools are already on the reserve list to shadow this additional Award next year.

Shortlisting

Riveting Reads

In February the Riveting Reads Book Award shortlist event is held at Ossett Academy. All participating school students are mixed into five small groups. Each group judges a selection of titles from the long list in order to identify one of the short listed titles for the Awards on each table. This promotes an energetic, passion driven discussion and much deliberation on judging books by their cover, readability, blurb and the best beginning.

The events are always great fun and organised by SLS team, the ECOT Co-ordinator and myself. Students then return to their own schools with a real reading buzz as Reading Ambassadors, promoting the Awards, its shortlist, our school's LRC and with a certificate and a highly sought after EOCT pin badge.

Julia Malcolm states *'My class are really excited about receiving our new box of books each half term. They also enjoy voting for their favourite books and finding out which ones have won.'*

Picture Book Award

The Picture Book Award shortlist event is held at an Infant School, students from each participating schools attend. As Lesley highlights *'the Picture Book shortlist process is very similar, but more informal. When the shortlist has been decided, the titles are read out to the students and they each vote for their favourite, using a token system. The outcome remains a secret until the big celebratory event in the summer.'* The SLS team have a key role in these proceedings and it is well received by all participating schools.

Deciding the winner

The SLS distributes two copies of each of the shortlisted titles to each school. All our students review the shortlist within their participating schools. In May the schools send in each student's vote and the overall winner is announced at the Award ceremony in June.

Lesley continues by stating that *'each reading group has more reading to do. There are certain activities the groups have to do, such as book reviews and writing to the shortlisted authors. This really does make a difference when we invite the shortlisted authors to the Book Award Ceremony – it's harder for them to say no when they've stacks of letters from students asking them to attend and saying how much they've enjoyed reading their book.'*

SLS contact the authors' publishers initially to pave the way for the official EOCT letter of invitation, author packs and student letters are sent out.

Award Ceremony

The Award Ceremony is held in June at Highfield School, a Special school for 11 to 16-year-olds, it is the climax to the shadowing process for both Book Awards. Any fantastic artwork, book reviews and other display worthy work by our students is displayed at the Award Ceremony.

All our school students, Book Club Co-ordinators, authors, the Master of Ceremonies, EOCT staff, SLS staff, Ossett Library staff are invited to the Awards. Our local book shop, Rickaro Books, is also invited to the event, which provides our students with the opportunity to support our local bookstore, by buying discounted books by the authors on the day. The books can be autographed and provide a lovely take away souvenir of the day.

Usually, the Picture Book Award is announced first by the Master of Ceremonies. This year it's Craig Bradley 'That Poet Bloke' on the podium. Although the Book Award is run on a shoe string budget we have been honoured to host some fantastic national and internationally renowned authors including: Linda Chapman, Ali Sparks, Joseph Delaney, Ellen Renner (who was my first ever house guest), M. G. Harris, and last year's winner Ciaran Murtagh.

In previous years authors have highlighted their enjoyment at seeing each school's presentation about their book at the Ceremony. This can take the shape of a book review, artwork illustrating an alternative book cover etc. Schools can be as creative as they like in their approach.

However, last year one of the schools acted out a scene from M. G. Harris's book *The Joshua Files* and we ended up on her blog! This was brilliant publicity and the students were grinning from ear to ear for weeks!

Lesley continues: *'SLS help on the day with Monica and the EOCT Team, getting the room ready, looking after authors, providing chocolates for authors and looking after the drinks table.'*

Whilst I liaise with the EOCT Co-ordinator, LRC's staff, SLS team, the Book Club Co-ordinators, publishers, authors, our appointed MC and bookseller, all the schools and our host at Highfield School turn each year's ceremony into a reality.

Our aim is to create an Oscars-style celebration of reading for all our students, to encourage students to view reading as a pleasurable, fun and engaging experience.

The Awards would truly not be such a success if it wasn't for those individual Book Club Co-ordinators who work tirelessly to promote, nurture and encourage reading and shadowing the Awards within each of the participating schools.

South Dale Primary School produce an exceptional personalised gift to each of the attending authors each year – a beautifully painted and crafted book cover, which is given to the authors as a parting gift. The winner is then announced and given a trophy and chocolates.

The authors then vacate the stage to and go to the signing tables and sign copies of their books or autograph books and talk to our very excited and enthusiastic students who patiently queue to see them.

As a parting gift to the students the Trust provides each school with a goody bag, which includes: bookmarks and a copy of the winning title for each school provided by SLS, posters, EOCT pin badges, certificates, autograph notebooks, pens and pencils for each student.

Next Year

Lesley states *'Every school involved says how much the children enjoy being part of the EOCT Book Awards. Students are eager to be part of the reading group and love reading brand new books and taking part in the shortlisting and Award Ceremony. Meeting the authors is the real highlight and so far we've been lucky, with at least three out of the five being able to attend. Long may that continue!'*

Finally, I feel as this is a child-led Book Awards, our students should have the last word , with this quote from a student at Dimple Well Infants School (who shadows the Picture Book Award):

> *'I love it when a new box of books arrives. I love it even more when my favourite story wins!'*

Students from South Parade School who shadow the Riveting Reads Award made the following comments today at their lunch time Book Club:

> 'It's amazing and fantastic and I would like to continue this in Year 6.'

> 'It's brilliant to finally share my passion of reading with others.'

> 'It's encouraged me to read other authors that I wouldn't normally read, we've learned that you can't judge a book by its cover!'

> 'I feel really special that I've been chosen to be a part of our school book club and represent our school, it's nice to socialise with other readers and know that my opinion counts and may make a difference to the author.'

Finally, a comment from Aiden Shields, one student who has participated in the EOCT/SLS Riveting Reads Book Awards twice (at Primary and also at Ossett Academy):

> 'I was able to explore books that I have never read through this scheme and meet my idol, Ali Sparks!'

Contributors

Lesley Hurworth is school librarian at Armthorpe Academy Doncaster with 875+ students including 120+ in the Sixth Form. Armthorpe is an ex-mining community. Lesley is also Chair of Doncaster Book Awards Ltd.

Lyn Hopson is school librarian at Don Valley Academy and Performing Arts College Doncaster, an 11–18 secondary school with approximately 1,170 students. Lyn is also Secondary Coordinator, Doncaster Book Award (DBA) Committee. The DBA is now 10 years old, with over 70 primary and secondary schools taking part.

Jean Corson is LRC Manager at Brayton High School, Selby an 11–16 smaller than average secondary school, whose shared values include 'Aim high to achieve our full potential.'

Paul Register is school librarian at Ecclesfield School, Sheffield, an all ability 11–16 school with approximately 1,720 students with specialisms in Visual and Performing Arts. He is the founder and organiser of the **Stan Lee Excelsior Award**, the only nationwide book award for graphic novels and manga where teenagers decide the winner.

Alison Roberts is Co-ordinator – School's Library and Resource Service, Discover, Calderdale Libraries.

> 'Discover has a menu of activities for children aged 4–11 years to encourage children to become active readers and find fun and interaction in the world of stories and imagination. Schools subscribing to our Discover education offer have access to a comprehensive range of services covering libraries, museums and arts.'

Jo Huett is librarian at Rossett School, Harrogate, an 11–18 Comprehensive School which converted to Academy Status on 1 July 2011. It has 1,500+ students on roll, including 280 in Sixth Form.

Pauline Thresh BA (Hons) MCLIP Is manager of the Leeds School Library Service, serving the needs of children and teachers across the city.

> 'Leeds Schools Library Service provides the best available resources direct to Leeds schools to underpin the curriculum, and inspire reading for pleasure in pupils and staff, raising attainment throughout the school.'

Lynne Coppendale PGDipIS MCLIP is librarian at Danum Academy Doncaster, a split-site 11–19 school with a library at each site, 1,550+ students including 400+ in Sixth Form.

Christine Hill is Principal Librarian at Hull Libraries. Hull City Council runs an active Schools Library Service providing excellent value, high quality resources, expertise and literacy engagement activities to support and work with school staff to encourage students to achieve their full potential to love learning and enjoy reading.

Monica O'Neill is the library resource centre co-ordinator at Ossett Academy & Sixth Form College in Wakefield, an 11–18 school with approximately 1,800 students on roll.

Lesley Marshall is Senior Cultural Officer at Wakefield Schools Library Service (SLS). SLS is a lively service offering a range of book loans and library exchanges, a Sound and Vision Library, advice and support, INSET talks, talks and displays, storytimes and material that can be selected by school staff or by library staff.